The ABRSM Practice Notebook

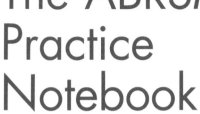

KU-432-680

Lesson Timetable

Lesson	Day	Time	Room	Other information
1 *SAMPLE*	20/05/08	10:40	MUSIC ROOM, B15	*SAMPLE* TURN UP 5 MINUTES EARLY AND BRING A PENCIL!
1				
2				
3				
4				
5				
6				
7				
8				
9				
10				
11				

Lesson	Day	Time	Room	Other information
12				
13				
14				
15				
16				
17				
18				
19				
20				
21				
22				
23				
24				

Lesson Timetable

Lesson	Day	Time	Room	Other information
25				
26				
27				
28				
29				
30				
31				
32				
33				
34				
35				
36				

Shopping List

Product title	Publisher	Price	ISBN No.*

* This is the unique number you find along the top of the barcode; it can help the retailer find the book for you and can be used to search on our online shop: www.abrsm.org/shop

TOP TIPS

Practising

1	Try to practise as regularly as you can
2	Plan your practice session before you begin it
3	Tackle short sections at a time
4	Work at the bits you can't play, not the bits you can
5	Practise slowly at first – only speed up when you can get it right
6	Later, practise your pieces right through and keep going even if you make a mistake
7	Concentrate and try to ignore any distractions
8	Include warm-ups, scales, arpeggios, and sight-reading each time you practise
9	Practise performing your pieces to your friends and family
10	Enjoy it! – every second spent practising makes you a better player

Concentrate and try to ignore any distractions

"Music is the thing of the world that I love most"
Samuel Pepys (1633–1703)

Sample Lesson

Things to practise

(YOUR TEACHER WILL WRITE DOWN HERE THE THINGS YOU NEED TO PRACTISE AND MAKE ANY COMMENTS ABOUT HOW YOU'RE PROGRESSING)

Effort: ☹ 1 2 3 ④ 5 ☺   Achievement: ☹ 1 2 3 4 ⑤ ☺

(staff lines)

Practice Diary*

Day	M	T	W	Th	F	W/end
How long?						

My comments

(TELL YOUR TEACHER OR PARENT/CARER HOW YOU'VE BEEN GETTING ON)

Parent's/carer's comments

(YOUR PARENT OR CARER CAN WRITE IN THIS COMMENTS BOX IF THEY LIKE)

Signature

* Why not place a sticker on each day that you practise?

"People who make music together cannot be enemies,
at least while the music lasts" Paul Hindemith (1895–1963)

Lesson 1 26th February

+ 7th March

Things to practise

Dozen a Day
pages 28 – 31

Riffs — b4 next lesson

Minuet in G   hands sep. + tog.

Effort: ☹ 1 2 3 4 5 ☺   Achievement: ☹ 1 2 3 4 5 ☺

Practice Diary*

Day	M	T	W	Th	F	W/end
How long?						

My comments

Parent's/carer's comments

Signature

* Why not place a sticker on each day that you practise?

"Music is music and that's it. If it sounds good, it's good music." Duke Ellington (1899–1974)

Lesson 2

Things to practise

Effort: ☹ 1 2 3 4 5 ☺   Achievement: ☹ 1 2 3 4 5 ☺

Practice Diary

Day	M	T	W	Th	F	W/end
How long?						

My comments

Parent's/carer's comments

Signature

"A musician cannot move others unless he is moved himself."
Carl Philipp Emanuel Bach (1714–88)

Lesson 3

Things to practise

Effort: ☹ 1 2 3 4 5 ☺   Achievement: ☹ 1 2 3 4 5 ☺

Practice Diary

Day	M	T	W	Th	F	W/end
How long?						

My comments

Parent's/carer's comments

Signature

"If I don't practice one day, I know it; two days, the critics know it; three days, the public knows it." Jascha Heifetz (1901–87)

Lesson 4

Things to practise

Effort: ☹ 1 2 3 4 5 ☺   Achievement: ☹ 1 2 3 4 5 ☺

Practice Diary

Day	M	T	W	Th	F	W/end
How long?						

My comments

Parent's/carer's comments

Signature

"We all have ability. The difference is how we use it"
Stevie Wonder (b. 1950)

Lesson 5

Things to practise

Effort: ☹ 1 2 3 4 5 ☺   Achievement: ☹ 1 2 3 4 5 ☺

Practice Diary

Day	M	T	W	Th	F	W/end
How long?						

My comments

Parent's/carer's comments

Signature

"Just don't give up trying to do what you really want to do. Where there is love and inspiration, I don't think you can go wrong" Ella Fitzgerald (1917–96)

Lesson 6

Things to practise

Effort: ☹ 1 2 3 4 5 ☺   Achievement: ☹ 1 2 3 4 5 ☺

Practice Diary

Day	M	T	W	Th	F	W/end
How long?						

My comments

Parent's/carer's comments

Signature

"Music is the language of the spirit. It opens the secret of life bringing peace, abolishing strife." Kahlil Gibran (1883–1931)

Lesson 7

Things to practise

Effort: ☹ 1 2 3 4 5 ☺   Achievement: ☹ 1 2 3 4 5 ☺

Practice Diary

Day	M	T	W	Th	F	W/end
How long?						

My comments

Parent's/carer's comments

Signature

"Don't play the saxophone. Let it play you."
Charlie Parker (1920–55)

Lesson 8

Things to practise

Effort: ☹ 1 2 3 4 5 ☺   Achievement: ☹ 1 2 3 4 5 ☺

Practice Diary

Day	M	T	W	Th	F	W/end
How long?						

My comments

Parent's/carer's comments

Signature

"After silence, that which comes nearest to expressing the inexpressible is music." Aldous Huxley (1894–1963)

Lesson 9

Things to practise

Effort: ☹ 1 2 3 4 5 ☺   Achievement: ☹ 1 2 3 4 5 ☺

Practice Diary

Day	M	T	W	Th	F	W/end
How long?						

My comments

Parent's/carer's comments

Signature

"Applause. The custom of showing one's pleasure at beautiful music by immediately following it with an ugly noise" Percy Scholes (1877–1958)

Lesson 10

Things to practise

Effort: ☹ 1 2 3 4 5 ☺   Achievement: ☹ 1 2 3 4 5 ☺

Practice Diary

Day	M	T	W	Th	F	W/end
How long?						

My comments

Parent's/carer's comments

Signature

"There are two means of refuge from the miseries of life: music and cats." Albert Schweitzer (1875–1965)

Lesson 11

Things to practise

Effort: ☹ 1 2 3 4 5 ☺   Achievement: ☹ 1 2 3 4 5 ☺

Practice Diary

Day	M	T	W	Th	F	W/end
How long?						

My comments

Parent's/carer's comments

Signature

"Without music, life would be a mistake."
Friedrich Nietzsche (1844–1900)

Lesson 12

Things to practise

Effort: ☹ 1 2 3 4 5 ☺   Achievement: ☹ 1 2 3 4 5 ☺

Practice Diary

Day	M	T	W	Th	F	W/end
How long?						

My comments

Parent's/carer's comments

Signature

TOP TIPS from tip-top musicians

1	Try to practise as regularly as you can
2	Practising a little and often is better than a long session once in a while
3	Remember to bring your instrument and a pencil to lessons or rehearsals
4	Listen carefully to what your teacher has to say and don't talk when they are speaking
5	Ask for an explanation if you don't understand something
6	Look after your instrument and keep it clean and protected
7	Carry spare strings (if you are a string player) and reeds (if you are a woodwind player)
8	Listen to lots of music – pop, classical, jazz – anything that interests you
9	Prepare and plan ahead – always have an ultimate goal in your mind
10	Enjoy yourself and believe in what you do!

Look after your instrument and keep it clean and protected

"Where words fail, music speaks."
Hans Christian Andersen (1805–75)

Lesson 13

Things to practise

Effort: ☹ 1 2 3 4 5 ☺   Achievement: ☹ 1 2 3 4 5 ☺

Practice Diary*

Day	M	T	W	Th	F	W/end
How long?						

My comments

Parent's/carer's comments

Signature

* Why not place a sticker on each day that you practise?

"Music expresses that which cannot be said and on which it is impossible to be silent." Victor Hugo (1802–85)

Lesson 14

Things to practise

Effort: ☹ 1 2 3 4 5 ☺   Achievement: ☹ 1 2 3 4 5 ☺

Practice Diary

Day	M	T	W	Th	F	W/end
How long?						

My comments

Parent's/carer's comments

Signature

"Music . . . can name the unnameable and communicate the unknowable" Leonard Bernstein (1918–90)

Lesson 15

Things to practise

Effort: ☹ 1 2 3 4 5 ☺   Achievement: ☹ 1 2 3 4 5 ☺

Practice Diary

Day	M	T	W	Th	F	W/end
How long?						

My comments

Parent's/carer's comments

Signature

"... music which can be made anywhere, is invisible, and does not smell." W. H. Auden (1907–73)

Lesson 16

Things to practise

Effort: ☹ 1 2 3 4 5 ☺   Achievement: ☹ 1 2 3 4 5 ☺

Practice Diary

Day	M	T	W	Th	F	W/end
How long?						

My comments

Parent's/carer's comments

Signature

"In memory everything seems to happen to music"
Tennessee Williams (1911–83)

Lesson 17

Things to practise

Effort: ☹ 1 2 3 4 5 ☺   Achievement: ☹ 1 2 3 4 5 ☺

Practice Diary

Day	M	T	W	Th	F	W/end
How long?						

My comments

Parent's/carer's comments

Signature

"I've never known a musician who regretted being one. Whatever deceptions life may have in store for you, music itself is not going to let you down" Virgil Thomson (1896–1989)

Lesson 18

Things to practise

Effort: ☹ 1 2 3 4 5 ☺   Achievement: ☹ 1 2 3 4 5 ☺

Practice Diary

Day	M	T	W	Th	F	W/end
How long?						

My comments

Parent's/carer's comments

Signature

"I can only think of music as something inherent in every human being – a birthright. Music coordinates mind, body, and spirit." Yehudi Menuhin (1916–99)

Lesson 19

Things to practise

Effort: ☹ 1 2 3 4 5 ☺   Achievement: ☹ 1 2 3 4 5 ☺

Practice Diary

Day	M	T	W	Th	F	W/end
How long?						

My comments

Parent's/carer's comments

Signature

"Great music is that which penetrates the ear with facility and leaves the memory with difficulty." Thomas Beecham (1879–1961)

Lesson 20

Things to practise

Effort: ☹ 1 2 3 4 5 ☺   Achievement: ☹ 1 2 3 4 5 ☺

Practice Diary

Day	M	T	W	Th	F	W/end
How long?						

My comments

Parent's/carer's comments

Signature

"There are more bad musicians than there is bad music."
Isaac Stern (1920–2001)

Lesson 21

Things to practise

Effort: ☹ 1 2 3 4 5 ☺   Achievement: ☹ 1 2 3 4 5 ☺

Practice Diary

Day	M	T	W	Th	F	W/end
How long?						

My comments

Parent's/carer's comments

Signature

"There's nothing to it: all you have to do is touch the right key at the right time and the instrument plays itself" Johann Sebastian Bach (1685–1750)

Lesson 22

Things to practise

Effort: ☹ 1 2 3 4 5 ☺   Achievement: ☹ 1 2 3 4 5 ☺

Practice Diary

Day	M	T	W	Th	F	W/end
How long?						

My comments

Parent's/carer's comments

Signature

"Over the piano was printed a notice: Please do not shoot the pianist. He is doing his best." Oscar Wilde (1854–1900)

Lesson 23

Things to practise

Effort: ☹ 1 2 3 4 5 ☺   Achievement: ☹ 1 2 3 4 5 ☺

Practice Diary

Day	M	T	W	Th	F	W/end
How long?						

My comments

Parent's/carer's comments

Signature

"Of all noises, I think music is the least disagreeable"
Samuel Johnson (1709–84)

Lesson 24

Things to practise

Effort: ☹ 1 2 3 4 5 ☺   Achievement: ☹ 1 2 3 4 5 ☺

Practice Diary

Day	M	T	W	Th	F	W/end
How long?						

My comments

Parent's/carer's comments

Signature

TOP TIPS

Preparing for exams

Aural tests

1 Sing back and clap tunes you've heard for the first time on radio or TV

2 Think about the key features in the music – where is it loud and where is it soft? Is it smooth or detached? What style is the music in?

Pieces and studies

3 Once you know a piece, practise performing it without stopping, even if you go wrong

4 Make sure you are familiar with the accompaniment, if your piece or song has one

Scales and Arpeggios

5 Practise your scales & arpeggios slowly and think about musical shaping before building up speed

6 Spot the scales and arpeggio patterns in the music you are playing

Sight-reading

7 Keep going in time to a pulse, even when you are just practising

| **8** | Plan how to use your half minute preparation time – try it out loud and clap the rhythms |

General advice

9	Listen to as much music as possible and go to live concerts whenever you can
10	Watch On Your Marks to see an exam in action – www.abrsm.org/onyourmarks
11	Don't leave any of your practice to the last minute!

Don't leave any of your practice
to the last minute!

"The audience is fifty percent of the performance."
Shirley Booth (1898–1992)

Lesson 25

Things to practise

Effort: ☹ 1 2 3 4 5 ☺   Achievement: ☹ 1 2 3 4 5 ☺

Practice Diary*

Day	M	T	W	Th	F	W/end
How long?						

My comments

Parent's/carer's comments

Signature

* Why not place a sticker on each day that you practise?

"After one has played a vast quantity of notes and more notes, it is simplicity that emerges as the crowning reward of art." Frédéric Chopin (1810–49)

Lesson 26

Things to practise

Effort: ☹ 1 2 3 4 5 ☺   Achievement: ☹ 1 2 3 4 5 ☺

Practice Diary

Day	M	T	W	Th	F	W/end
How long?						

My comments

Parent's/carer's comments

Signature

"Music has charms to soothe a savage breast, to soften rocks, or bend a knotted oak." William Congreve (1670–1729)

Lesson 27

Things to practise

Effort: ☹ 1 2 3 4 5 ☺   Achievement: ☹ 1 2 3 4 5 ☺

Practice Diary

Day	M	T	W	Th	F	W/end
How long?						

My comments

Parent's/carer's comments

Signature

"What is best in music is not to be found in the notes."
Gustav Mahler (1860–1911)

Lesson 28

Things to practise

Effort: ☹ 1 2 3 4 5 ☺   Achievement: ☹ 1 2 3 4 5 ☺

Practice Diary

Day	M	T	W	Th	F	W/end
How long?						

My comments

Parent's/carer's comments

Signature

"I hate complacency. I play every gig as if it could be my last, then I enjoy it more than ever." Nigel Kennedy (b.1956)

Lesson 29

Things to practise

Effort: ☹ 1 2 3 4 5 ☺   Achievement: ☹ 1 2 3 4 5 ☺

Practice Diary

Day	M	T	W	Th	F	W/end
How long?						

My comments

Parent's/carer's comments

Signature

"The most perfect technique is that which is not noticed at all." Pablo Casals (1876–1973)

Lesson 30

Things to practise

Effort: ☹ 1 2 3 4 5 ☺   Achievement: ☹ 1 2 3 4 5 ☺

Practice Diary

Day	M	T	W	Th	F	W/end
How long?						

My comments

Parent's/carer's comments

Signature

"There is no top. There are always further heights to reach." Jascha Heifetz (1901–87)

Lesson 31

Things to practise

Effort: ☹ 1 2 3 4 5 ☺   Achievement: ☹ 1 2 3 4 5 ☺

Practice Diary

Day	M	T	W	Th	F	W/end
How long?						

My comments

Parent's/carer's comments

Signature

"I do not consider my self as having mastered the flute,
but I get a real kick out of trying." James Galway (b.1939)

Lesson 32

Things to practise

Effort: ☹ 1 2 3 4 5 ☺   Achievement: ☹ 1 2 3 4 5 ☺

Practice Diary

Day	M	T	W	Th	F	W/end
How long?						

My comments

Parent's/carer's comments

Signature

"It is a mistake to think that the practice of my art has become easy to me . . .
There is scarcely a famous master in music whose works I have not frequently
and diligently studied." Wolfgang Amadeus Mozart (1756–91)

Lesson 33

Things to practise

Effort: ☹ 1 2 3 4 5 ☺   Achievement: ☹ 1 2 3 4 5 ☺

Practice Diary

Day	M	T	W	Th	F	W/end
How long?						

My comments

Parent's/carer's comments

Signature

"A bit of nerves is a good thing. If it overwhelms and paralyses you, it's a bad thing. You have to get the right balance." Jo Brand (b.1957)

Lesson 34

Things to practise

Effort: ☹ 1 2 3 4 5 ☺   Achievement: ☹ 1 2 3 4 5 ☺

Practice Diary

Day	M	T	W	Th	F	W/end
How long?						

My comments

Parent's/carer's comments

Signature

"There is no feeling, except the extremes of fear and grief, that does not find relief in music." George Eliot (1819–80)

Lesson 35

Things to practise

Effort: ☹ 1 2 3 4 5 ☺   Achievement: ☹ 1 2 3 4 5 ☺

Practice Diary

Day	M	T	W	Th	F	W/end
How long?						

My comments

Parent's/carer's comments

Signature

"Music, a magic far beyond all we do here."
J. K. Rowling (b. 1965)

Lesson 36

Things to practise

Effort: ☹ 1 2 3 4 5 ☺   Achievement: ☹ 1 2 3 4 5 ☺

Practice Diary

Day	M	T	W	Th	F	W/end
How long?						

My comments

Parent's/carer's comments

Signature

Holiday Practice Diary

Week beginning

Day	M	T	W	Th	F	W/end
How long?						

Week beginning

Day	M	T	W	Th	F	W/end
How long?						

Week beginning

Day	M	T	W	Th	F	W/end
How long?						

Week beginning

Day	M	T	W	Th	F	W/end
How long?						

Week beginning

Day	M	T	W	Th	F	W/end
How long?						

Week beginning

Day	M	T	W	Th	F	W/end
How long?						

Week beginning

Day	M	T	W	Th	F	W/end
How long?						

Week beginning

Day	M	T	W	Th	F	W/end
How long?						

Week beginning

Day	M	T	W	Th	F	W/end
How long?						

Week beginning

Day	M	T	W	Th	F	W/end
How long?						

Week beginning

Day	M	T	W	Th	F	W/end
How long?						

Week beginning

Day	M	T	W	Th	F	W/end
How long?						

TOP TIPS

Why do music exams?

1 Exams give you a goal to work towards

2 Exams help you measure your progress

3 Your certificate is a reward for all of your hard work

4 Exams provide a useful performance opportunity

5 Examiners are professional musicians who offer useful feedback to help you to progress further

6 ABRSM exams are recognized and respected throughout the musical world

7 Everyone who passes an ABRSM exam can be proud of their achievement

Everyone who passes an ABRSM exam can be proud of their achievement

Essential Theory

Time values: notes and rests

Notes	Rests	
o	▬	semibreve or whole note
𝅝	▬	minim or half note
𝅘𝅥	𝄽	crotchet or quarter note
𝅘𝅥𝅮	𝄾	quaver or eighth note
𝅘𝅥𝅯	𝄿	semiquaver or 16th note
𝅘𝅥𝅰	𝅀	demisemiquaver or 32nd note

NB a dot after a note makes it longer by half its value:

𝅘𝅥. = 𝅘𝅥 + 𝅘𝅥𝅮   𝄽. = 𝄽 + 𝄾

Time signatures

$\frac{2}{4}$ means two crotchet (quarter-note) beats in a bar

$\frac{3}{4}$ means three crotchet (quarter-note) beats in a bar

$\frac{4}{4}$ means four crotchet (quarter-note) beats in a bar. It is sometimes notated as 𝄴 'common time'

$\frac{2}{2}$ means two minim (half-note) beats in a bar

$\frac{3}{2}$ means three minim (half-note) beats in a bar

$\frac{4}{2}$ means four minim (half-note) beats in a bar

$\frac{3}{8}$ means three quaver (eighth-note) beats in a bar

$\frac{6}{8}$ means two dotted crotchet (quarter-note) beats in a bar

$\frac{9}{8}$ means three dotted crotchet (quarter-note) beats in a bar

$\frac{12}{8}$ means four dotted crotchet (quarter-note) beats in a bar

Staves and clefs

Treble clef	Bass clef	Alto clef	Tenor clef

Letter names of notes

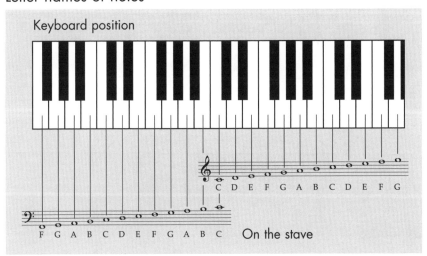

Keyboard position

On the stave

Sharps, flats and naturals

♯	sharp
𝄪	double sharp
♭	flat
𝄫	double flat
♮	natural

Circle of 5ths and key signatures

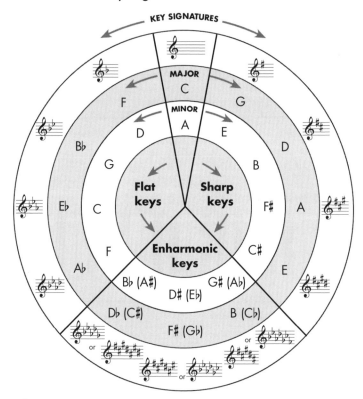

Dynamics

pp (= *pianissimo*)	very quiet
p (= *piano*)	quiet
mp (= *mezzo piano*)	moderately quiet (literally 'half' quiet)
mf (= *mezzo forte*)	moderately loud (literally 'half' loud)
f (= *forte*)	loud
ff (= *fortissimo*)	very loud
◁————	= *crescendo* (or *cresc.*) gradually getting louder
————▷	= { *decrescendo* (or *decresc.*) / *diminuendo* (or *dim.*) } gradually getting quieter

Tempo markings

accelerando (or *accel.*)	gradually getting quicker
adagio	slow
allegro	quick (literally 'cheerful')
andante	at a medium ('walking') speed
lento	slow
moderato	moderately (allegro moderato: moderately quick)
presto	very fast
rallentando (or *rall.*)	gradually getting slower
ritardando (or *ritard.* or *rit.*)	gradually getting slower
ritenuto (or *riten.* or *rit.*)	held back
tempo	speed, time (a tempo: in time)

More terms and signs

cantabile	in a singing style
da capo (or D.C.)	repeat from the beginning
dal segno (or D.S.)	repeat from the sign
fine	the end
legato	smoothly
mezzo	half (*mezzo forte*: moderately loud)
poco	a little
staccato (or *stacc.*)	detached
	a tie joins notes of the same pitch
	over two *different notes* (not to be confused with a tie) or over a group of notes is called a 'slur': perform the notes smoothly
8va	means: *ottava* (octave)
8va	(over a note or notes): perform an octave higher
8va	(under a note or notes): perform an octave lower

TOP TIPS

Exam day

1	Warm up at home or school before the exam
2	Arrive at least 10 minutes early and use this time to get your instrument and music ready
3	Once in the exam it's OK to warm up with a scale, or a few bars of a piece
4	Feeling nervous is completely natural and can actually help you focus
5	Tell your examiner whether you'd like to start with scales or pieces
6	Begin when you are comfortable and ready
7	Don't worry about pauses between your pieces, the examiner is just writing and will tell you when to move on
8	If things go wrong KEEP GOING and don't worry about mistakes
9	Don't be afraid to play out loud during your half minute preparation time

10 Remember that the examiner is on your side. They appreciate the hard work you have put in to prepare for your exam

Feeling nervous is completely natural

End of Year Report

Aural skills

Pieces and studies

Music theory

Scales and arpeggios

Sight-reading

Other musical activities

Summary comments

Signature   Date

Manuscript

Manuscript

Notes

Notes